Inspire To Act

Jennifer A. Borislow
Mark S. Gaunya

STRATEGIC VISION
PUBLISHING

www.inspiretoact.com

Jennifer A. Borislow Insurance Agency, Inc

Strategic Vision Publishing
1 Griffin Brook Drive
Methuen, MA 01844
www.strategicvisionpublishing.com

ISBN: 978-0-9825459-0-4

Table of Contents

The Power of Kindness

A simple act of kindness can brighten someone's day. It can be what that person remembers about that day, what that person talks about. More often than not, it will inspire a person to act, to carry forward the beauty of that moment. One simple act can create a chain reaction of shared acts of kindness — that is what this book is all about.

Consider the people who cross your path each day — family, friends, co-workers, grocery clerks, a gas station attendant, a barber or a hairdresser. Each contact, no matter how fleeting, presents an opportunity to make a difference. It can be as simple as the words you choose, the smile you shine or a quiet gesture you make. When you are guided by your heart in each of your daily encounters, you are more present in the moment, more in tune with the people you meet and more connected to the world around you. This is among the greatest gifts you can give to others and to yourself.

"If your actions inspire others to dream more, learn more, do more and become more, you are a leader."
— John Quincy Adams

Inspiring others to act begins with doing for others. Positive connections with people have a direct impact on how we feel about ourselves. Sharing that feeling with others creates a wonderful spirit and enthusiasm that is both contagious and powerful.

How It All Began for Us

We are partners in a successful business, built over 30 years and very much centered on people rather than on products or services. Attracting the best talent to our team and creating a culture of caring have always been hallmarks of the way we do business. While we have numerous team events throughout the year, we always try to make the holidays extra special.

Several years ago, we were discussing holiday gifts for our dedicated team, a subject that sparks lively conversations every holiday season. *Should we give a gift basket or a gift certificate? Would our team members like a gift that we pick out or one that they get to pick themselves? How much should we spend? What do they really need? What do they want? What are they expecting?* Somewhere in the course of the conversation it became clear that our favorite gifts, the ones we will never forget, had been both unexpected and out of the ordinary. And those gifts shared two other important traits: they exemplified kindness and caring, and they made our team say, "Wow, you didn't have to do that."

That conversation led us to decide to do something very different that year. In place of the customary gifts for our team, we started a tradition called "random acts of kindness." Little did we know that our gift that holiday season would have a profound impact on our team members, ourselves and, ultimately, on our company's culture. It has gone on to touch people and places far beyond what we could have imagined or ever intended. We can't take credit for that; the process seemed to take on a life of its own. Our decision to do something different was one simple act that created a chain reaction of shared acts of kindness.

This book shares those stories of random acts of kindness. People borrowed ideas from one another and applied creativity, joy, and caring to create a ripple effect and amplify the goodwill they had witnessed. The stories of these acts of kindness have touched our hearts and inspired us to share them with you.

May these stories touch your heart, enrich your soul and inspire *you* to act.

Random Acts of Kindness: The Rules of the Game

Before we dive into the stories, we need to answer two of the most common questions we are asked about random acts of kindness: "What are they?" and "What rules apply to making them happen?"

The great Louis Armstrong changed the world by revolutionizing and energizing American music. He was once asked by an interviewer to define jazz. He answered, "Man, if you gotta ask, you'll never know." Like jazz, two great things about kindness are that we know it when we see it and that it's at its best when we improvise.

What typifies random acts of kindness?

- They can be delivered in any denomination … monetary, emotional or physical.
- They are often spontaneous and unexpected by the recipient.
- They may be shouted from the rooftops or performed in total anonymity for any reason you choose.
- They may involve total strangers, casual acquaintances or those we know well.
- They help those in need. Whether that need is a smile, a meal, a helping hand, an inclusive spirit or a roof overhead, kindness knows no upper or lower limits.

- They are among the only things that you can simultaneously keep and give away, because they are a gift both to the recipient and to the giver.
- They may have the power to change the world or a single life, but all they have to do is brighten just one person's day.
- They may be personal acts for oneself or acts of leadership that say to anyone watching "Look at how good this makes us feel … you can do it too."
- They are contagious and transformational to those around you.

So what are random act of kindness all about? It's up to you. It's all about your gratitude, creativity, spontaneity and joy. Although we can define a few guidelines that we have employed, we don't pretend to offer any sort of rulebook. We don't know the limitations of gratitude, kindness or creativity, so we cannot offer a list of dos and don'ts.

The stories in this book are all true as reported by our team members, colleagues, friends and those they have inspired to perform random acts of kindness. Their names have been removed to protect their privacy.

Chapter 1: The $100 Question

"You can't live a perfect day without doing something for someone who will never be able to repay you."
— John Wooden

In 2008, we decided to change our holiday gift-giving theme and do something different for our team. We called it "random acts of kindness." We kicked it off by asking our team a question: If you had $100 to give away to someone else, what could you do with it in order to make a difference in the life of another person?

We gathered our entire staff in our cafeteria space and presented each person with an envelope. The room was buzzing with anticipation as everyone opened their envelopes. Inside they found a letter and a $100 bill. The letter included a request to perform a random act of kindness before the date of our holiday party and instructions on how to go about it. The rules were simple: find a person or people whom you don't know, and use this money to make a difference in their lives. And one more thing — at the company holiday party, you will be asked to share your random act of kindness with your teammates.

Each team member left the room excited and energized with thoughts of what he or she could do. In the following days, we heard the conversations in the hallway as the team shared ideas. The excitement was building.

Each team member viewed the assignment differently and completed it in his or her own way and with a specific purpose in mind. Lives were touched, differences made. Wow! The stories our team shared at our holiday celebration were simply amazing. Here are a few examples as told by our team members:

• My son was so intrigued by this opportunity that he wanted to participate with me. Together we came up with a plan. I took him to the florist and we purchased 25 poinsettias. We then went to a local Haven Home and delivered them to individuals who will not have visitors during the holiday season. It brought both of us great joy to see the smiles on the faces of the recipients, and it was a wonderful lesson for my son.

• I sent five separate donations to St Jude's Children's Research Hospital in honor of five of my mentors. I took the time to write a personal note telling them how special they were to me and about the donation I had made in their honor.

• My stepbrother is in Afghanistan. I know how much he appreciates receiving mail and figured others who are deployed there feel the same way. So I sent 100 cards to Holiday Mail for Heroes. Each was personally signed. The money paid for the cards and postage.

• I went to the local coffee shop and stood in line with half of the money. As I got closer to the counter, I started listening to what people were ordering and began paying for their orders one by one. They couldn't believe it! I then asked the manager to use the remaining $50 to pay for as many drive-through orders as it would cover, and I was on my way.

- I split the money into $20 bills and placed each randomly in five hymnals in the pews of my church so that five parishioners would discover them during the Christmas season. I included a note explaining that it was a random act of kindness. It was their choice of how they chose to use the money. If they needed it, they were welcome to keep it, or they could place it in the offering tray or choose to give it to someone else who might need it more.

- I go out of my way to get my gas at a local gas station, as they are always so friendly and accommodating. There is a young mechanic who always seems to have his head under the hood of the car and doesn't usually say much. I learned that he is a student at a local university and works every available moment to pay for his education. He has a limited social life, as making money is his main priority. I chose to make his day by giving him a note with the $100 that told him to go out and have fun.

- I take the train to work every day and make the 15-minute walk from my house. On my way, I pass many homeless people, and one of them always makes eye contact with me. We say hello without ever saying anything else. One day, I decided to invite him to follow me to the local convenience store so I could buy him lunch and a gift card. Then I took him to a nearby clothing store to buy him a new coat. Now when we pass each other I know I made a difference, because I can see him wearing his new coat.

The gift that keeps on giving

What started out as a new idea to "get into the spirit" of the season turned into a holiday tradition that the team would thoroughly embrace and incorporate into their daily lives. The "viral effect" this new tradition created is life-changing. It has become "the gift that keeps on giving."

Chapter 2: Opportunities for Everyday People

"You can observe a lot just by watching."
— *Yogi Berra*

People present opportunities for kindness every day. It is so easy to become absorbed in the complexities of our work, family and social issues that we lose ourselves in a narrow focus. The job, the kids' activities, the "to do lists," the latest email, tomorrow's tough meeting — despite it all, the world continues to spin in the present, bringing with it opportunities to make a difference.

Being present and sharpening your senses in search of opportunities for random acts of kindness can be a life-changing experience. It puts you much more in the moment because you are tuned in to the people around you — looking, listening, sensing emotion and appreciating interaction in ways you may not be used to. It makes it easy to discover opportunities for random acts of kindness among the people we encounter every day.

The following stories are personal accounts of his random acts of kindness:

The Nutcracker "sweet"

Once a month I get my hair cut at a local salon, and I always enjoy the feeling of "freshening up." It's not really newsworthy — in fact, it's pretty ordinary — but one of those visits ended in tears of joy that touched my heart.

Alicia, my hairdresser, is a hardworking single mom with a teenage daughter whom she adores. When I visit, we always catch up on life, family, friends and current events. This visit was different.

It was early December, and Alicia was telling me about her plans for the Christmas holiday. She told me how she loves this time of year because it is all about family, friends, festive decorations and being grateful for all that life has to offer. She also shared that she had saved up enough money to buy her daughter an iPhone. She was very excited to give it to her, not only because her daughter wanted it, but also so she could stay better connected to her. As the father of three teenage children, I could totally relate to her excitement on both levels.

Alicia also told me that her daughter was a ballet dancer, and second only to the cellphone, her holiday wish was to see Tchaikovsky's The Nutcracker, which is performed every year in spectacular fashion by the Boston Ballet. She wanted to take her daughter to see it. But she couldn't afford both the ballet and the phone. Alicia was struggling to find a way to tell her daughter, though she knew she would be deeply disappointed. I listened and didn't offer any suggestions. I knew exactly what that conversation would sound like … and it wouldn't end with a smile.

When my haircut was finished and we were standing at the cash register, I was thinking about how hard Alicia works, how hard raising a teenage daughter on her own must be and how torn she was over her dilemma. I paid Alicia for my haircut and then pulled her aside to share a random act of kindness. My tip was enough money for her to take her daughter to The Nutcracker in Boston. Her eyes filled with tears, and she didn't know what to say. I told her there was no need to say anything; just enjoy the show and make some special memories. I don't recall the details of the remainder of that workday … but I will never forget the deep satisfaction I got from the look in Alicia's surprised eyes.

Summer in the City of Brotherly Love

On a business trip to Philadelphia, I took a cab from the airport to the hotel — an ordinary thing to do on an ordinary day. The cabdriver's name was Rodney, a 65-year-old man full of energy and enthusiasm for life. Rodney greeted me with a big smile and a warm welcome to the City of Brotherly Love. We exchanged small talk about the day and life in general, and during our conversation, he mentioned the summer barbeque he throws for 100 underprivileged inner-city kids.

Rodney reached into his weathered leather briefcase on the seat next to him and pulled out some documents about the certified nonprofit organization he founded and was proudly running for inner-city kids. He told me the challenging economy was making it hard to pull together the supplies necessary to run this year's event. With just under a week to go, he was concerned about it all coming together. He reassured me (and really, himself) that he would be resourceful and figure it all out. As he said, "The universe always provides." That saying really resonated with me, because it was the same thing my mom used to say to me when I was growing up.

Rodney had grown up in the inner city, and he told me how hard it was for his mom to make ends meet. He said life was especially challenging during the hot summer, with school out and limited options to get relief from the heat or have any fun. It was his life experience that inspired him to act and make a difference to 100 kids in the city — kids just like he used to be – and for one day to take them out to enjoy a day at the park with all the fixings.

When he dropped me off at the hotel, I told him about our random acts of kindness and reached into my wallet to pay him his fare along with some extra cash to buy the supplies he needed for this year's summer event. Rodney's face lit up, and again he reached into his briefcase to show me the list of things he needed for the barbeque. He said with another big smile, "With your help, I can get all these items, stop worrying about how I was going to pull it all together and focus on creating some magic for the kids — this is a gift bigger than you know." He shook my hand, we parted ways, and I walked away safely delivered and with a brighter smile on my face, knowing Rodney was able to provide those kids with some summertime relief.

A bone-chilling experience

In my hometown there is a full-service gas station on a corner of downtown Main Street. It's not fancy, and it doesn't come with all the "bells and whistles" of full-service, brand-name gas stations. But it's staffed with guys who always have a smile on their face as they're just trying to earn a living, to pay the bills.

New England winters can be a challenge. It gets snowy and cold — sometimes bone-chillingly cold. One day I pulled into the gas station on my way to work and was greeted by Joe. Now, Joe's scruffy beard may be in need of some grooming, but he always greets you with the warmest smile possible. No matter the weather, Joe always wore mid-length jean shorts, a vest, no gloves and a pair of brown, weathered boots. On this stark winter day the mercury read one degree below zero — just looking at Joe in his shorts made me shiver inside my warm car. I got the usual warm greeting, and I asked him, "Aren't you cold?"

He said, "Not really. I ate a good breakfast this morning, and that's keeping me warm!"

I watched him fill up my car and do the same for a couple of other customers with the same positive energy I had come to know and respect.

Joe told me the total, and I handed him my credit card. He returned with the slip for me to sign, and I handed him back the clipboard with the signed receipt along with enough cash to buy some winter work pants. Joe tried to push the money back and said he couldn't take it. I said, "Please, go buy yourself a warm pair of pants ... you are making me cold just watching you." We both laughed, he took the money, and when I saw Joe again a week later — he was wearing a new pair of long pants.

Sometimes it's easy to forget that basic necessities can be a challenge for some people even when they are working. This simple, random act of kindness made a big difference to Joe and warmed my heart in the process.

Fueling kindness

I work in downtown Haverhill, Massachusetts, where I park in a municipal garage. It's not exactly the safest place, but I'm observant, alert, and comfortable moving in and out. One day, as I walked from my car to the elevator, I noticed a car with the hood open and two kids standing next to it. As I walked by I shouted out, "Need any help?" to which they said, "No, all set." I kept walking, and as I rode the elevator to my office floor I thought to myself, Are they really all set, or can I actually help them? I shared my exchange with the receptionist, and together we went back to the garage, where the kids were still standing. We asked what seemed to be the problem, and they told us they had run out of gas and were waiting for a friend to come help, as they didn't have any money. I grabbed my phone and called AAA to bring gas for their car. Then I gave the kids some money. They were stunned, and with tears in their eyes they said, "This is the nicest thing anyone has ever done for us."

A world turned upside down

Two boys from our town lost their father when he died in his sleep, the week after Christmas. He was just 39 years old. Ever since, the mom has struggled balancing her new life without her husband and working long hours to make some additional money to cover some of their household expenses. She was focused on trying to pick up the pieces of her family's life after this traumatic change. My family and I treated the boys to a day in Boston at the circus as well as dinner and a sleepover afterward. This provided the mom the opportunity to have a day and night "off," to be alone and relax. It felt so good to see the boys smile and a mother reenergized after a good night's rest.

These stories underline the tremendous power of habit. Giving back whenever we can is so rewarding that doing it again and again becomes a wonderful habit. Fortunately, it turns out that good habits are just as hard to break as bad ones are. Spontaneous acts of kindness are born out of these good habits: observation and listening.

Chapter 3: Ladies Night — From Networking to Making a Difference

"Carry out a random act of kindness, with no expectation of reward, safe in the knowledge that one day someone might do the same for you."
— Diana Spencer, Princess of Wales

Once we experienced the power of random acts of kindness in our own company culture, we began to share the joy with others in our personal and professional lives. One of the special events during the holiday season is a gathering of a remarkable and talented group of businesswomen. What started as a company networking group soon became a social group that fosters open dialogue and the sharing of business successes and challenges. The events planned for this group quickly earned the nickname "Ladies Night" and have become evenings that we all look forward to several times a year.

Ladies Night is a great combination of interesting people, wonderful themes and great locations for our time together. We have done some fun things, such as cooking and painting classes and going to the theater, to concerts and to theme dinner events. But the holiday celebration is always special and held at home. With a desire to make the holiday evening inspirational, we decided that we would extend our corporate philosophy of random acts of kindness to this ladies' networking group.

Each of the women received by mail an elegantly gift-wrapped box decorated with a bright bow and jingling bells. The box included instructions that fully outlined the random act of kindness activity along with a $100 bill to assist them in that task.

What happened next was quite touching. Our phone began to ring, and emails started coming in. One consistent question emerged: Can we do more? These leaders had the means to increase the $100 starting point, and, in fact, they all matched or increased it significantly in performing their own random act of kindness. Another remarkable thing happened ... the very few in the group who did not readily see the power of our company's random act of kindness cultural norm soon understood its power when they practiced it themselves as part of the Ladies Night group. The experience opened their eyes to how they could spread the spirit to their families, their friends and their companies. In doing so, some discovered an untapped and powerful source of leadership by example and realized the opportunity to instill this cultural norm in their companies — an exponential impact for sure.

The first time we gathered to share our experiences of what each of us did with the $100-plus was magical. We laughed, we cried and we all listened eagerly to how the others went about spreading the spirit of random acts of kindness. In subsequent years, we have continued with random acts of kindness, and the stories remain just as remarkable. We share some of them here.

It's the little things

When I received a beautifully wrapped package with a tiny jingle bell fastened to the lovely bow, I opened it with great anticipation and read carefully the letter of instruction with the crisp $100 bill. As a successful CEO and business owner, I was surprised at my own level of anxiety.

My immediate reaction was to do something that had significance and that I would be proud to share when I came together with the other ladies who are a part of this special group of women.

Where to begin? I asked many people, including my children, for suggestions, and all offered up many wonderful ideas — everything from paying for groceries and buying gifts for needy children to donating to various charities.

On my way home from work one night, I stopped by a local homeless shelter and walked in for the first time. I spoke with the director, showed her my letter and asked her if I could help someone at the shelter. She immediately offered many suggestions and then told me about a young woman with two small children who had arrived at the shelter earlier that morning. She shared some of her background story and suggested some simple items, such as toiletries and small gifts for her kids.

I left the shelter and headed to Target, where I bought all the items she suggested, spending way more than $100 but feeling fulfilled that I was going to make a difference in a stranger's life.

I returned to the shelter with all the items in a few gift bags and left them with the director. She was touched by my thoughtfulness and thanked me profusely. I told her that there was no need to thank me and that what I did was easy. I thanked her for what she does every day.

Random acts of kindness are a wonderful reminder that each of us has the capacity to give and touch the lives of others. Sometimes we need to be reminded that it takes only a little effort. Thank you for awakening my holiday spirit.

Rosie's Place

Every year, our company partners with Rosie's Place, a sanctuary for poor and homeless women in Boston, to provide warm coats, hats, scarves and gloves to their residents. We also donate toys to their "toy shop," where the women can choose Christmas presents for their children. Because it's such a busy time for everyone at our company, a colleague and I generally do the shopping for our team. It was a wonderful feeling to have an extra $100 to put toward the cause. So many of the items requested are small things that we take for granted and buy on a whim without even thinking about the cost — journals, family games, lotions, sports apparel, etc. The extra money went a long way to make the holiday a little better for families in transition. The stories everyone shared when we all came together were really inspiring. I was touched by the thoughtfulness, caring and creativity that each and every person put into where the money would go, and by how they impacted a group or individual and what it meant to each of them.

Special delivery

What do you do when someone gives you $100 and asks you to do a random act of kindness? I started by searching "random acts of kindness" on the Internet and was amazed at the stories I read online. I thought, I want to make it a meaningful gift, and I want it to touch someone who hardly gets recognized and can use the money. I decided to choose the person I work with who delivers the mail every day from floor to floor with a smile and a nod. I wrote a note thanking him for doing his job so well, included the $100 and suggested that he take his wife out to dinner. He was overwhelmed and speechless. I had no idea that he and his wife lived in a small apartment with their four kids. They had a simple life, and going out to dinner was rare and always a special treat for the family. He sent me an email thanking me and sharing that he would be taking his entire family out to a special Christmas dinner. He added that my gift has taught his children that generosity exists and emerges when you least expect it. Now every time he walks by my office and drops the mail in my bin, he has a big smile and pep in his step.

Laughing all the way
to the food bank

When I got my assignment, I asked many people what they would do — whom they would select and how they would distribute the money if they had the chance. I even discussed it with my children and got their input. Engaging others in a thoughtful conversation has been the greatest gift of all. I ended up selecting a local food bank after seeing an article on how food was short this year and how many people would not receive an appropriate amount of food and would suffer from malnutrition. I took a partner in crime, my mother, and we went to the grocery store, filled up multiple carriages and delivered it all to the food bank.

Charity begins at home

There are so many people in need and so many wonderful people who take care of elderly residents. They are not paid much, but they love their work, and knowing that their help makes a difference is worth more than a paycheck sometimes. I chose to recognize a few of the home health aides who go above and beyond to support the residents of my nursing home. I wrote several thank-you notes, put the money in the cards and gave them to the home health aides. I wanted them to know how much I appreciate the work they do and the difference they make in the residents' lives. It was a simple yet effective way to say, "Thank you."

Just have it altered

At 4' 10" I am constantly having my clothes altered. Pants and skirts are too long, so I take them to my favorite tailor to be shortened. I've been there many times and don't really know much about the elderly woman, other than that she is very pleasant and does not speak any English. Recently, I learned that she works two full-time jobs — a total of 80 hours per week.

It is clear that the small shop is a family affair. Often I see her grandchildren in the back room, sitting at a table doing homework or just hanging out. This time when I picked up my new pants, I decided to give her an extra tip — a crisp $100 bill. She looked puzzled and handed it back to me, saying, "No, no, no." I knew she thought I was paying for my pants, but I pushed it back at her and said, "Merry Christmas." Her eyes filled with tears, and she graciously nodded her head and said, "Thank you." I left the shop in tears myself … knowing that I had made a difference that day. The feeling touched my heart, and it was wonderful.

Teachers are amazing role models

I shared the idea of the random acts of kindness with my friend, a third-grade schoolteacher. She loved the idea so much that she had the students in her classroom do random acts of kindness for each other. They learned that doing for others was easy and rewarding. The kids were creative, as they had no money or pretense of how to perform their kind acts. They helped clean out desks, shared a snack, made a card, wrote a note, hung up a coat, volunteered to erase the blackboard and many other school-related tasks. The lesson was more powerful than the physical act. The practice of kindness should be a daily habit. The teacher shared with her students that the power of kindness is twice blessed. It blesses the one who gives with the feeling of being helpful, and it blesses the person who receives with a feeling of gratitude.

For a special child

My niece, Casey, is a fourth-grade special-needs schoolteacher who is passionate about education and her special kids. The children in her class have overcome incredible odds. I spent my $100 purchasing gifts for one of the students, who was recently diagnosed with a very rare condition. She has undergone multiple surgeries in a short period in the hope that these procedures will prolong her life. I shared this story with my card group, and several people stepped forward, matched the money, and volunteered to go with me to pick out the gifts to give to the child and her family. It was an amazing experience and a great feeling not only to provide for this child but also to multiply my gift with the generosity of others.

Too close to home

I overheard a conversation at work about a teacher whose son was friendly with my son when they were in school. Out of the blue, her son was diagnosed with a brain tumor and has a limited time to live. I knew him well; I actually worked with his father in my former profession. I was stunned, and my mind drifted to how I could help this family — what can I do? I decided that maybe I could help with food and a few meals. So I drove to the store, purchased some groceries, went home and made several meals. While I was out shopping I also picked up some gift certificates for takeout food places. I put the meals and the gift certificates together and drove to the teacher's house. I rang the doorbell and when she appeared at the doorstep- I handed her the basket. She was surprised and very appreciative.

A serving of kindness for the lunch lady

A school cafeteria worker in our building is a single mom raising two kids. She has a sunny personality and is always very positive. Recently, she had knee surgery, which will keep her out of work and without a paycheck for six weeks. She delayed the surgery as long as possible, knowing that it was going to be a very challenging time for her family. I solicited the help of a friend to find out more about her children's Christmas wish list. Then I braved the midnight crowds on Black Friday to purchase holiday gifts for the entire family. Knowing I was shopping for a special family with a hardworking mom made the craziness of the seasonal shopping more enjoyable. I had a purpose, and it was exciting to know that I was helping someone else. The gifts were delivered anonymously, and the entire experience has given me great joy.

Giving thanks

I chose to share this wonderful opportunity with my extended family over the Thanksgiving holiday. Before I could even get the food on the table, my entire family was pooling their money. We spent Thanksgiving discussing how we could collectively have the greatest impact with the money we collected. We chose a local food bank. That weekend we went out and stocked their shelves with products they desperately needed. The simple homework assignment of selecting someone to receive the $100 turned into an amazing family affair and a donation of more than $370 in food. This will become an annual Thanksgiving tradition for our family.

The Ladies Night tradition continues. It has prompted some in the group to extend random acts of kindness to other spheres in their own lives. And so the momentum builds. We frequently get notes such as this one from the ladies: *I am looking forward to the holiday Ladies Night and to hearing all the wonderful stories. That is one of the highlights of the experience. When we all sit around and tell what we have done, it provides a window into everyone's beautiful heart. I don't have words to express the feelings that it evokes, but I do know that I am a better person because I have learned how to be more generous.*

Who could ask for more?

Chapter 4: The Ripple Effect

"The reports my team gave brought more tears to my eyes than I've shed in years. Each time I read them I tear up again. Wouldn't it be something if each family in America (the 'ripples') would do this and that the kindness would grow to a point where we don't have the political fights our nation now faces? I have no idea how to fix America, but perhaps this can be a beginning."
— *E. Dennis Zahrbock*

Have you ever tossed a pebble into a lake when the water was completely calm? The pebble may be small, but the effect it makes can be significant. From that tiny "plop," ripples spread out in all directions. That tiny pebble can affect an area thousands of times its size, casting beautiful rings in the water as the effect spreads across the still waters of the lake.

The same expansive effect occurs when you do something nice for someone else. It starts with one small act and eventually initiates many other small acts. Each tiny act of kindness has the same beautiful ripple effect: wave after wave of positive impact.

Because we decided to share stories with many of our colleagues, remarkable things have happened. Many have started similar traditions and generated their own ripple effects within their families and communities. What a wonderful gift! In the stories that follow, one simple act created a chain reaction of shared acts of kindness.

A little goes a long way

When my daughter-in-law went into labor, I knew it would be a great opportunity to find a recipient for my random act of kindness. But instead of one single act, I divided up my $100 and soon found out that a little goes a long way.

The first part went to a sweet hospital housekeeper. I let her know that we definitely appreciated her thankless job — and wished her a merry Christmas. The next went to a labor and delivery nurse who maintained vigilant duty throughout her 12-hour night shift while we all tried to wait patiently for this baby to arrive. She was hesitant to accept it but then replied with gratitude, "Well, I'll just pay it forward!"

My last act was the most noteworthy. I met a woman in the ladies' room, where she was fumbling and panicked about not finding something in her purse. She seemed desperate, so I asked her why she was at the hospital. She said that her father had suffered a heart attack and she had just arrived. She rushed to get there and realized that she had forgotten her wallet at home. In her nervous state, she said, "I don't like to be without my wallet." I knew I was there at the right time, and I offered her the remaining money from my random acts of kindness. It was enough for her to feel she had some money if she needed it. She hugged me with tears in her eyes. Life is a blessing, and every day is a gift. Wake up each day and spread that blessing around! *I will definitely be watching out for more opportunities.*

Anonymous thoughtfulness

The city I live in has put in new parking meters, and the parking rules are still a little fuzzy. So I stuck enough money to cover one parking ticket under the wiper of a car that had a ticket. The envelope simply said, "Merry Christmas."

I decided to turn toward my little community and help some people on my block. The Salvation Army has a homeless shelter/rehab facility very close to my condo. As part of the program, clients are required to work at the warehouse and help out around the neighborhood to offset the cost of treatment. A lot of people don't know this, and these men are often seen in a poor light. So I decided to purchase 10 pizzas and just drop them off at the center. My goal was to just bring a little cheer and say, "Hey, someone notices what you are doing and hopes that each day you gain strength to overcome your challenges."

What we tend to forget is that not all good things you do need to be praised openly. The gift of just knowing you did something good for someone else is priceless. In the end, I hope it keeps them wondering and thinking, *what can I do to pay this back?* And maybe they'll even pay it forward.

Opportunities are everywhere

My gifts began with my donation to "Double the Pot Day" at the Salvation Army Red Pot. As I walked by, the bell ringers were cheerful and full of joy. Most days I rush by, but this time I noticed a sign stating that any donation received on that day would be matched by a local business. Perfect!

The next day, as I drove down the same street I have driven down every day for the past 15 years, I noticed something that I hadn't fully appreciated before. My neighbor has an adult son with special needs. On this particular day I noticed that the family may have had trouble with the upkeep of their home. There was a Metro Mobility bus in front of the house and my neighbor was standing in the walkway waiting for his son. As I drove by, he gave me the most wonderful smile and a big wave as if to say, "Hello, have a great day." That simple gesture made an impression on me. , so I turned around, got out of my car and gave him money to buy his family dinner. He was quite shocked and very appreciative. It taught me a valuable lesson. When you open your heart, you see what's around you every day and notice things you haven't seen before. *Take time to notice the little things and all the beautiful people who make our world a better place.*

A most welcome envelope

I decided to wait for situations to present themselves and, rather than overthinking it, go with my instincts. I printed little cards with the Wikipedia definition of a random act of kindness and put one in each of five envelopes along with $20. My method was to place the envelope in front of the recipient, say, "Merry Christmas," and then dash off.

My first gift went to a family of five while they were dining. I noticed that they were very selective on the menu, with the kids sharing an item. So when we were ready to leave, I presented the envelope to the mom and said it was especially for her. She looked puzzled and said "For me?" and I said, "Merry Christmas," and left.

I presented the next one at a local store to a mother with three kids, one of whom was in a wheelchair. I gave her the envelope, again saying, "Merry Christmas," and left. These acts of kindness were bringing tears to my eyes!

The third was presented at a coffee shop when the barista gave me my tea and said, "Be careful, because this is going to be delicious!" She made me giggle, so she got an envelope and a "Merry Christmas." The fourth one was at the gas station, where it was very random. I left it on a car window for a cheery surprise upon the owner's return to the car.

The last one was at the mechanic. When he was finished, I reached out my window to give him the envelope, and he kept saying, "No, thank you." I insisted and made him read the card. He read it with tears in his eyes and said he had heard of this happening before and couldn't thank me enough.

I will continue this wonderful tradition; I printed a little Christmas newsletter of my own and am sharing this with more than 20 family members. *Instead of material things this year, I am giving the gift of this same experience. I choose to believe that there is more good than evil in the world, and I think doing this makes the world a little brighter — wow!*

The gift of music

My grandma passed away this year. I wanted to do something in her honor and for the other folks who live at the nursing home that cared for her. My favorite client from work has a spouse in the same nursing home, so I called the nursing home and found out what they needed for their holiday celebrations. The home has a New Year's Eve celebration at noon (because they cannot manage to stay up until midnight), and they have never had live music. I negotiated with a quartet that I auditioned for my wedding — they loved the idea and agreed to cut their fee by about 80%. I matched the random acts of kindness money and hired the band to play for a couple of hours as the seniors joyfully rang in the new year.

Chapter 5: The Currency of Kindness

"In life you can never be too kind or too fair; everyone you meet is carrying a heavy load. When you go through your day expressing kindness and courtesy to all you meet, you leave behind a feeling of warmth and good cheer, and you help alleviate the burdens everyone is struggling with."
— Brian Tracy, motivational author

Having some money to conduct your random act of kindness is great, but the joy, goodwill and ripple effects you can create by doing random acts of service are just as valuable. Offering our time, expertise or tools, or even just a hand to hold, are all ways we can give for free that deliver immense value.

Looking for opportunities to put kindness front and center in your life can lead to some of the simplest and most powerful acts of kindness imaginable. It would be easy to underestimate them and say, "Well, anyone would do that." But it's not just a question of doing the right thing when the obvious course is placed before you. Random acts of kindness are all about intention and habit, about being on the lookout all the time for even the simplest actions.

A cynic might say, "So you helped an old lady across the street; what do you want, a medal?" But these actions add up. They become a bank of goodwill in the universe. And even when you think they are not observed, they inspire others to act, and that is the gift that keeps on giving — an exponential impact that is almost impossible to measure.

- When out running errands, we find ourselves looking for opportunities to perform random acts of kindness. We pick up trash and move objects out of the road. We found the contents of a woman's wallet, including her license and credit cards, scattered over the road and mailed them back to her. While we are working on our physical wellness, we are also doing little good deeds along the way to work on our spiritual wellness.
- A nurse I know works nights at the hospital. I made extra dinner one night so I could take some to her during her shift. She thought it was so great not to have to eat in the hospital cafeteria.
- It was raining. I was walking my dog, and a family stopped me to ask for directions because their car broke down and they needed to know how to get to the dealership to pick it up. I walked my dog home, got my car and drove them there.
- I carved pumpkins for a fund-raiser this weekend. One of the young girls there loved the pumpkin I carved, so I let her keep it.
- Today was trash day in my neighborhood. I noticed that my neighbor had left for work but had forgotten to take his garbage can to the curb. So I did it for him. When he got home, he

came over to thank me. It made me feel pretty good.

- On a recent flight, there was a boy about 10 years old seated next to my husband and me. He was traveling alone with his little sister, who was two rows ahead. It was their first time flying. I gave up my seat so they could sit together and then traded again with my husband so he didn't have to babysit the whole flight!
- We were at the arcade this weekend, and I noticed a girl about 10 years old who was there alone, staring at all the games. She obviously didn't have tokens, so I gave her a handful of ours. She was very grateful and so happy.
- We were walking down toward the beach, and a group in front of us, which included an elderly woman, was walking slowly in the sand. They were all carrying a lot of beach stuff. Even the older woman was carrying a large L.L. Bean bag. I grabbed the heavy bag, carried it for them and helped someone else in their party with an umbrella. It was a simple thing for me to do to help a stranger have a better day.

It is no surprise that random acts our team members conduct without money are equally as touching as the ones that involve cash.

Chapter 6: Hand in Hand — A Day of Service

"Too often we underestimate the power of a touch, a smile, a kind word, a listening ear, an honest compliment or the smallest act of caring, all of which have the potential to turn a life around."
— Leo Buscaglia

The many demands on your time and attention can be overwhelming. It's easy to lose sight of what's important — such as taking time to say thank you and giving back to your community by expressing an attitude of gratitude. Every year we put a new twist on our company tradition of a random act of kindness. But the theme — giving back — is recurring.

For 2013, our random act of kindness was a community service day just before our company holiday event. It was designed to help our nonprofit clients save time and money and to help our team members make a difference.

Our organization is honored to be the strategic advisor to quite a few nonprofit clients, and we reached out to them to see how we could help. We picked six clients to work with and then organized our employees into service teams to volunteer their paid work time to travel to and from our clients' worksites. Our staff completed various tasks such as painting classrooms and bathrooms, decorating Christmas trees, putting up holiday decorations, and running errands. One of the many benefits of this year's event was the opportunity for us to pair up employees who normally don't get the chance to spend time together, and this event turned out to be a great team-building opportunity as well.

The feedback from our clients and employees was heartwarming — and to us, what life is really all about. A nursing home client we helped said, "Our deepest gratitude and appreciation for the service your team provided to us last Wednesday ... The health center looks beautiful with all the Christmas trees and decorations. Our residents and team leaders had fun making the button bracelets we will sell to raise money for charity at our fair on Friday. It was such a fun and energetic group to work with. That was definitely a random act of kindness."

One of our employees said, "Wanted to take a minute to thank you for the wonderful day yesterday. What a great experience and a nice way to end the day with our holiday celebration and the day of service sharing. I am truly grateful to work with such a caring group of people."

With all the challenges we face on a daily basis, it's easy to lose sight of what's truly important — it's the people we serve and the difference we make. If you share our tradition of giving back and living an attitude of gratitude, we know that you have experienced the same ripple effect in your life that we have in ours.

Chapter 7: Leaving a Lasting Impression

"It is up to each of us to decide what sort of impression we will leave in our path and whether the sum of our actions will resonate for a moment or last for the lifetimes of those we help and support."
— *Bob Feldman, management consultant*

When you are in the moment and aware of what's going on around you, it can take you outside of your comfort zone. Seizing the opportunity to do something nice for another person creates a chain reaction of positive effects. The more you act, the more you inspire others to act, the greater your impact on the world ... and on yourself. Ironically, people who have developed this habit and experienced the satisfaction that it brings report that the biggest beneficiary of random acts of kindness is the giver because of the joy that gratitude brings!

We can create an impact — or feel one — in innumerable ways. Here are some of them:

- I experience mixed emotions when I am invited to perform random acts of kindness. At first, I am stressed as I struggle with the question "What am I going to do?" I have learned that I can't wait until the last minute to come up with my idea and perform the random act. That anxious feeling dissipates as soon as I do something special for someone else. The deep satisfaction and joy more than make up for the stress I put on myself.

- I thoroughly enjoy sharing the stories. I wish I could be as creative with my ideas as some of the others are, but at the same time, I realize that each and every act is special in its own way. Performing random acts of kindness has reinforced that great reward can be achieved when we push ourselves beyond our comfort zone.

- I am amazed by the creativity that emerges as we help others.

- I am awed by the various acts, and it makes me feel so good to know that people truly care about others.

- There is a sense of community and pride that one's generosity makes a difference.

- I love the way new ideas that make a lasting impression on others stay with me always.

- I truly believe that people can make a change in someone's life by performing random acts of kindness.

The following stories were shared with us by the recipients of random acts of kindness.

Office elves

A co-worker found a surprise note and a gift card to the local supermarket on her desk when she arrived at work. Her family had some financial challenges, and the holidays would be tough this year. The random act of kindness made a huge difference. The note was signed *Your secret elves.*

In response, the recipient, not knowing who left her the gift card, wrote the following and put it on the office notice board, where she was sure that the right people would see it: *To the special person(s) who made a difference in my life … I can't begin to thank you for your generous "elves" gift. It really brightened my day as well as my husband's. Although there have been many bumps along the road, it really makes you realize that people really do care and you aren't in this all alone. I don't think I will ever find words that can express that feeling.*

A little pick-me-up
goes a long way

Traveling back and forth to the hospital each day to spend time with her mother, whose health had been failing for months, was starting to take its toll on the daughter. In a random act of kindness, a note, a meal and a gas card were left at her house. The recipient wrote in response, *I wish there were a way in which I could truly show my appreciation not only for your generous gift but also your kind words in your note. Some days you really need that little bit of encouragement to give you a lift, and that is what you did for me. Thank you both very much from my husband and myself. I wish you a very happy holiday season and New Year.*

A dark hour before dawn

It had not been a great year for our family. Certainly other people had troubles far worse than ours, but somehow when you're living through tough times, the down times always seem just a little bit lower than the next guy's.

In mid-November, my husband's company had a large layoff, and he was not spared. One month later, we learned that he had prostate cancer and surgery was his best bet. Now, Christmas was almost here, and with three small children under the age of 10, we were doing our best to rise to the occasion and have the Christmas spirit, even if it often meant faking it.

One morning, as I was rushing out the door to put the kids on the school bus, I noticed an envelope under the windshield wiper of our car. I didn't have time to get it until after I had come back from the bus stop, which was probably for the best, because when I got back and opened the envelope, a tear came down my cheek that certainly would have provoked many questions from curious children. A $100 bill was in the envelope. The note simply said, *Merry Christmas.*

An overwhelming feeling of *this world really is full of wonderful people, and I am so, so lucky to know one of them* came over me. Over the next few weeks, the wheels in my head could not stop spinning ... Who on Earth would have done this? Who was so kind ... yet didn't leave a name so I could thank him or her? Even after I asked a few close friends, the mystery was not solved.

Then, a couple of months later, I figured it out by accident. My wonderful neighbor asked what I did with my $100. As soon as her question came out, she realized she had spilled the beans, and she felt so bad for letting it slip. I then realized the money had come from her daughter-in-law. I learned that she worked for a very generous employer that gave each of its employees $100 that was to be given to whomever they chose as a gift in the form of a random act of kindness ... My angel decided to give it anonymously.

I put the envelope and money away for a time when we might really have need for it. Now its five years later, my husband and I are working, he is cancer-free, our children are growing into lovely ladies, and I have decided that the $100 should be given to somebody who needs it far more than we do.

Thank you to the angel who picked me and to your company for starting the ball rolling. The angel who left the money will probably never understand what her generosity meant to our entire family. Although the money has switched hands, the generosity of the person who passed it to us will always be remembered.

If the shoe fits

A friend's wife was in a terrible accident and had a long road to recovery. She mentioned on her Facebook page that her favorite pair of boots was destroyed in the accident. We purchased a pair of the boots and sent them to her. Here's the text of the handwritten note we received:

A special package arrived today ... relatively anonymously. Lisa spent her first night at home last night, and it was really good for her. She went back to her parents' house tonight, and she found the boots in the package. I know you had something to do with this random act of kindness, so thank you. I will hold out as long as I can before telling her whom they are from. Thank you. You made my wife smile again.

A beautiful tribute on the ice

Friends of mine lost their son recently at the young age of six. Their mission now is to spread love, healing and kindness in his memory. At about the same time, another young boy who played hockey with our kids also lost his battle with cancer.

While at the hockey rink watching the boys practice, a random act of kindness was bestowed on me. A woman who was a stranger to me handed me a very nice gift bag and said, "I want you to have this." And then she was gone. I imagined that she might be watching me from afar, but I couldn't see her. In the gift bag was a photo of a young boy on a rocky New England beach, his arms spread wide and a look of pure joy on his face. It noted that at bedtime the boy would often say, "Today was the best day ever." It suggested that if people showed more kindness every day, the world would be a better place.

The bag also included tickets for our sons to attend a special professional hockey game played in the boy's honor. It asked only that I perform random acts of kindness in the community and gave a few simple examples. The beauty and elegance of this gesture were truly moving to me and a great example of creativity in random acts of kindness. And what an amazing tribute to two special boys gone way too soon!

Chapter 8: Kindness in the Wake of Disaster

"You cannot do a kindness too soon, for you never know how soon it will be too late."
— Ralph Waldo Emerson

Desperate moments come in many forms, public and personal. Some we share as a nation. Some we suffer as a family. Some we must cope with alone. The power of kindness is no antidote to tragedy, but it is perhaps the most soothing way to ease some of the pain.

When tragedy strikes, many of us immediately look for ways to help. We forget the trivial things and refocus on what we can do for those who have been impacted by the tragedy. It is often said that in the toughest times our true nature reveals itself and we adopt an attitude of "we are in this together". The spirit of random acts of kindness enables us to respond thoughtfully and with agility. Our team employs the culture of kindness to provide a rapid response to the violence of nature, the despicable acts of a few evil people, and even the tragedy of family loss and illness. Kind, thoughtful messages and acts of kindness inspire us to be better, more compassionate and even more humble.

The Sandy Hook shooting, Newtown, Connecticut

As parents, we watched in horror the tragedy of the Sandy Hook Elementary School shooting in December 2012. No one can imagine how an ordinary day could turn into such a nightmare.

In the days following the tragedy, like so many others, we were looking for ways to help.

Inspired to spread good in the world, Ann Curry, the anchor of NBC's Today show, asked viewers to perform 26 random acts of kindness, one for each of the people killed at the school. It became a movement to honor the victims, and it spread quickly throughout the world. It gave grieving people something to do, as they felt helpless and heartbroken for the victims and their families. Suddenly, everywhere you turned, you would hear of so many other tributes to the Sandy Hook victims.

My oldest daughter was quick to embrace this challenge and inspired others to follow. She purchased 26 Starbucks gift cards and placed them on random cars in the mall parking lot with a note that read, to honor the 26 people who died in Newtown, Connecticut, I am doing 26 acts of kindness. You are number 3. I hope you have a wonderful holiday season. God bless!

Other examples included:

- 26 lottery tickets were handed out to perfect strangers.
- 26 toys were donated to local Toys for Tots charities in honor of the 26 victims.
- 26 candy bars with notes were left at a local nursing home.
- 26 McDonald's gift certificates were given to 26 children at a local YMCA.
- 26 Thank you for your service notes were left at a local veterans' home.
- 26 thank-you notes were left for police officers, firefighters and emergency responders.

Superstorm Sandy

When Hurricane Sandy hit, the turmoil it caused that portion of our country was terrible. We learned that it had affected an employee of one of our valued clients, and we wanted to do something to help. It was right before the holiday season, and every year as a business we sponsor less fortunate children by buying Christmas presents for them and their families. This sparked an idea: the affected employee was a New Jersey mother of twins who lost everything she had in the storm. We all thought, *how could she possibly begin to think about buying Christmas gifts for her two young children, especially with all that they need to replenish?* We decided to put our holiday gift efforts toward this family and give them a Christmas that would be more memorable than the tragedy they were struggling through.

We came together, and the donations from each of our employees kept coming and coming. And the week before Christmas, we shipped her 14 toys for each child and $965 in gift cards — for a grocery store, Home Depot, The Children's Place, Target, Toys R Us and Walmart — for their family to start their rebuilding process. Words can't truly describe how we felt when we heard from the client and the employee after she received the package.

She sent us a photo book of the kids opening their presents on Christmas Day, with a note that read:

Words cannot express how grateful and appreciative we are for what all of you did for our family. It warms my heart to know there are people like all of you in this world. After the storm, I was not myself and basically was walking around in a daze. I could not get into the Christmas spirit, but then I was told that your company wanted to help and sponsor Christmas. That was a big weight lifted off my shoulders. I was in awe when the box arrived. I couldn't believe my eyes! All I kept thinking was "WOW." There is no way that we can thank you enough. We are truly grateful. Someday when we are in a better position, we will be sure to pay it forward and help others in need as well. So, to all of you – thank you, thank you, thank you from the bottom of our hearts.

The Boston Marathon bombing

Two of our employees were running the Boston Marathon in April 2013 when terrorists set off deadly explosive devices near the finish line. The results were three fatalities and many severe injuries, including severed limbs. The remarkable responses of the first responders, the runners, the hospitals and the Boston public were evidence of an indomitable spirit and a city well prepared for the worst. "Boston Strong" still rings loud and clear as the new motto of an old and historic community. Fortunately the explosion did not physically injure Michele and Shaina, as they were forced to stop running a half a mile from the scene. But like the thousands of spectators near the scene and those of us watching from afar, they were affected deeply and emotionally.

The outpouring of professionalism and support that came from the Boston Athletic Association following that day was both courageous and encouraging. This inspired Michele and Shaina to act — to do something for the B.A.A. in an effort to thank the association for all it had done for the runners, the injured, the survivors and their family members. These two women reached out directly to the association, asking if there were something they could do to help. Ten days later, the ladies traveled back to Boston, their feelings still raw from Marathon Day, to the B.A.A. office, just a short walk away from the scene of the heinous act of terror and the finish line they never got to cross. They assisted in organizing, packaging and shipping hundreds of boxes to runners who were forced to leave their personal belongings behind that day. While it was the least they could do, it offered a bit of closure for them, and the association was grateful for their help.

Coming together in the wake of disaster represents a bittersweet dichotomy of sadness and hope. We have learned that when grief is raw and hearts are heavy, you can make a difference with the simplest of gestures- whether spoken, written or an unselfish act of support. The healing process is made a little easier by responding with kindness and love.

There can never be an antidote for the cause of tragic events. It is when tragedy occurs that there are powerful opportunities to strike a blow for the good. It is the ideal moment to make a statement, stand up and make a difference.

Chapter 9: For the Person Who Has Everything

"Never doubt that a small group of thoughtful, committed citizens can change the world. Indeed, it's the only thing that ever has."
— Margaret Mead

What do you give to the person who has everything? Consider that this accomplished person is not seeking material gifts but would be far better pleased and honored by an act of kindness inspired by and dedicated to him or her. Perhaps there is someone whom you want to acknowledge, but not by simply buying a gift.

I was deeply moved when this was done for me. An event held in my honor was turned into an evening of amazing stories of random acts of kindness. The invitation read: *No gifts, please. Use the money you might have spent on a gift to do a random act of kindness, and be prepared to share at the celebration event.* At the gala celebration, one by one each attendee shared his or her personally selected random act of kindness in recognition of my years of service to a wonderful organization.

The evening was magical. The stories and kindness shared that evening were incredible, and the lives they touched were truly heartwarming. It was one of the greatest gifts I could have ever received. No material gift would ever trump the feeling that we all felt as the random acts were shared, one right after another.

Here are a few of the stories:

• The evening started with a story of education and helping kids who could not afford the luxury of new school supplies. Steve shared the story of his son, who attended a private school, where many of the students were on financial aid. Purchasing extra school supplies was not in their budget, so Steve purchased several backpacks with his son, filled them with supplies and gave them to the teacher to give to the students who needed them most.

• The next story shared was centered on women in leadership and how they can be role models. The words of praise were touching, and as a parent of daughters I found it a great message for young girls. Tony's daughter, Lindsey, is a dance movement physical therapist who works with autistic kids and uses dance as a form of therapy. Lindsey is a role model, and the kids she helps look up to her as a friend, confidant and mentor. Tony's random act of kindness was through the charity that Lindsey works for — he paid for several children to participate in dance therapy classes.

• Vancouver, British Columbia, is pretty cold in the wintertime. Penny is passionate about helping the homeless and spends much of her free time volunteering at the homeless shelter. What the homeless people love most is getting new clothes.

Street people rarely have warm clothing and hardly ever receive something new. Penny and Jim purchased two dozen long-sleeved shirts and gave them to the homeless.

- The Chesapeake Children's Museum of Annapolis, Maryland, specializes in providing kids an opportunity to learn about the environment. Each year the organization holds a gala event to raise money to continue its mission of educating and providing kids a safe place for after-school child care. This year a table of people will be enjoying the gala celebration in my honor. And I'm very honored indeed to know that my name will be associated with such a great cause.

- Youth Homes, a not-for-profit organization with the motto "We never give up on a kid", is a place that surrounds young people with the support and attention they need to reach success in life. Regardless of where they come from, whether there is abuse in the home or trafficking on the street, Youth Homes helps bring an end to the bad cycle. In California there are three homes. Mark and his wife decided to take 12 kids and two staff members to a holiday celebration — a performance of A Christmas Carol and dinner out — a very special evening.

- At a high school in South Bend, Indiana, the budget was so tight that providing new basketball sneakers to the team was not a priority. An avid sports fan, Scotty knew that he could fix that problem, so he decided he would help encourage the team to another successful season by surprising them with a random act of kindness: new basketball sneakers for the entire team.

Why not honor someone in your circle or community in the same way? It may take some organization, but the joy and satisfaction it yields will be well worth it ... guaranteed.

Chapter 10: Serving Those Who Serve with Honor

"We can't help everyone, but everyone can help someone."
— Ronald Reagan

Sacrifice, courage, and selflessness are the essence of what our men and women in uniform do every day to protect our lives and liberties. When we speak about various random acts of kindness and the myriad of wonderful gestures performed, we never want to lose sight of helping those who are already heroes. Our men and woman in uniform are heroes and role models, and a "thank you" may never truly express the depths of our gratitude, but performing a random act of kindness for our women and men in uniform is a great place to start.

Appreciation is defined as "the recognition and enjoyment of the good qualities of someone or something." Below are a few stories in which that appreciation transcends a simple thank-you. Whether large or small acts, they send the message that we appreciate the service of our people in the services and that they are very much in our hearts and thoughts.

Selfless service and a
need to provide

It's all about the shoes! Have you ever heard that saying before? In this case it's not about buying that new pair of shoes you always wanted; instead, it's about keeping the shoes you already own in tip-top shape with a professional shoeshine.

On a business trip to Washington, D.C., I noticed my shoes were in desperate need of a shine. So when I checked into my hotel, I spotted a shoeshine chair and an energetic middle-aged man working hard to satisfy another customer. When it was my turn, I jumped in the chair and was greeted by a big smile, a passionate "Hello!" and an assurance that I was going to get the best shoeshine I had ever had in my life.

"That's a tall order," I said with a smile back at him, to which he said, "Have you ever had your shoes shined by a 20-year Marine Corps veteran?" I said no, and he said, "Sit back and relax, young man. You are in for a treat!"

His name was Steve, and he was a veteran of the Iraq war, serving three tours of duty. He also was the father of six kids and the proud owner of five shoeshine stands like the one I was sitting in that morning. Steve was passionate about his work, and it showed in the way he went about his business. He was also passionate about his kids and struggling to make ends meet. Steve lost his wife tragically to a senseless act of violence. She had been murdered while he was on his last deployment in Iraq.

Steve wasn't looking for any sympathy. Quite the opposite — he was totally focused on giving me the best shoeshine ever ... and by accident he gave me a little more. Steve touched my heart with the story of his family and how they were all working hard to overcome the loss of their wife and mother. He shared that he was proud of his kids for going to school and helping him around the house in addition to working part-time jobs so they could help him make ends meet. He also told me with pride in his eyes how well his business was doing, giving people like me the best shine ever. Amazingly, Steve never complained about his life challenges, but you could see the pain in his eyes as he shared his story.

When he was done giving me the best shoeshine ever, I told him about a tradition my business partner and I started many years ago called random acts of kindness. That's when I handed him his shoeshine fee along with some extra cash and said with a smile, "You are an amazing father and a passionate business owner, and you have served our great country as a Marine. Thank you." His eyes watered up from our exchange, and he shook my hand and looked at me in a way I will never forget.

Serving our country

Our military men and women, police officers, firefighters, and other first responders serve our great country and communities with honor and pride. Their dedication and sacrifice should be rewarded with our gratitude.

For as long as I can remember, the desire to thank our servicemen and -women has been a feeling that runs deep. As a business owner who travels frequently, I run across them quite often. Usually it's in the hallways of an airport or in a restaurant or pub located in the terminal. When the opportunity presents itself, I offer to pick up the check or just say, "Thank you. Thank you for your service to our great country. It is because of people like you that my family and I feel safe and secure. Thank you for that gift of safety and for making a difference in our lives and many others all over the U.S."

These gestures of gratitude are usually met with a sincere thank-you and a humble smile followed by "You're welcome; it is my privilege." And sometimes, they are met with a warm handshake and a look in the eye that tells you the gesture meant more to them than the drink or meal. For me, that is the real reward.

Chapter 11: Are You Inspired to Act?

"Kindness is the language which the deaf can hear and the blind can see."
— Mark Twain

When you become inspired to act, you not only touch the life of the recipient of our action, but you may inspire others to act as well. Encouraging others to commit random acts of kindness anywhere — in the workplace and schools, within the community, and even at home — is a start toward making a difference in many lives. Through random acts of kindness, it seems that our personal beliefs in genuine empathy for others have also become the guiding principles of our business. It has become the bedrock of our corporate culture. Sharing with other organizations ways in which they might create a similar cultural norm is also part of our random acts of kindness tradition.

The image of a snowball getting larger as it rolls downhill comes to mind when we reflect on our journey so far and where we are today. With so many new and exciting ways to inspire others to act, we continue to be amazed at the creativity and joy people bring to the tradition of random acts of kindness. Listening to, reading about and witnessing those around us as they share their stories brings to life a new perspective on human nature and a joy in the knowledge that kindness is contagious.

If reading these powerful stories elicits emotions, feelings and a sense of purpose, we hope it inspires you to act and make a difference in someone's life. Perhaps your own random acts will include offering this book to a colleague, peer or friend. Maybe you will just leave a copy out somewhere publicly so others may be inspired to act too. There's no limit to kindness.

Above all, we hope you will share stories of your acts of kindness and inspire others to do so as well — it's often called *paying it forward*. If you are a leader, consider making it part of the culture of your organization or group. We highly recommend doing so and assure you, the return on that investment is beyond your imagination.

Chapter 12: Getting Started

"The way to get started is to quit
talking and begin doing"
-Walt Disney

Now that you are inspired to act, we're sure you're wondering, "What's the best way to get started?" It couldn't be easier. Here are a few things we recommend that you keep in mind and a few examples of key phrases that we have used to communicate the important ideas:

1. Help people understand what you're talking about and define your terms. What do you mean by a "random act of kindness"? We used the actual definition from Wikipedia when we introduced the idea to our team. We do the same with friends and family.

    Wikipedia describes a random act of kindness as a selfless act performed by someone to either help or cheer up a stranger, for no reason other than to make people happier. Random acts of kindness can be either spontaneous or planned in advance. Extraordinary acts of kindness are wonderful gifts.

    For further insight, please see "Rules of the Game" in the Introduction section of this book.

2. Make sure you express your thankfulness and appreciation to the people you are inspiring: your

team, colleagues, friends or family. Take a moment to mention the joy you feel in being surrounded by such good people.

Example: *We have a great appreciation for all you do throughout the year, and to celebrate the holiday season we will once again be asking you to create your own extraordinary act of kindness for someone else — to brighten that person's day.*

3. Tell people clearly what you want them to do and what resources you have provided. That might be money, time or some other commodity that makes it easier for them to act.

    This is an example from one of our holiday random acts of kindness events: *In the past, you have received money toward performing your random act. This year, there is a twist. This is your invitation to perform your own extraordinary act of kindness with an act of service — and without involving money at all. This may involve a little extra thinking — or maybe not — but it will greatly show that some random acts of kindness are worth far more than any money you can spend.*

4. Set some ground rules, and suggest a time and parameters. This is important to allow everyone to share ideas and be ready to tell stories about their acts and the outcomes.

    Example: *You will have until Thursday, December 15, the day of the agency party, to perform your extraordinary act of service. Be ready to share your experience at the holiday celebration.*

5. Tell some stories about what others have done, to stimulate ideas.

    These are examples from one of our events where we encouraged people to perform random acts of kindness without the use of money:

    - Gift of time and laughter: Make someone laugh and smile, share a funny story, brighten someone's day with some joy
    - Gift of a written note: Send a thank-you note or write a letter to an old friend, or just send a card to say hi
    - Offer to help clean or decorate a house or run errands for someone in need or struggling
    - Take on some responsibility for someone so he or she can enjoy a night out or some personal time
    - Make a dish or bake something, and deliver it to someone's house unannounced at a time of need

6. Remind people of your cultural norms and traditions and of what sets your company, your family or your group of friends apart. Esprit de corps and pride are important motivators and uniters. That's one reason random acts of kindness are among the best team-building and bonding activities imaginable.

Example: *At Borislow Insurance, the mission is to make a difference in the lives of our clients, their respective families and one another. We are blessed with continued success, and it represents the cumulative effort, dedication and hard work contributed by each of you! This is another way to give back and help others through our own teamwork and spirit.*

7. Above all, make it fun and keep it lighthearted. Assure people that the return on their investment of time and caring is enormous and that they can really make a difference.

8. One easy step you can take is ... *to share this book with your employees, colleagues, friends and family!*

We hope you get started right away. And we hope you will send us stories about your random acts of kindness at stories@Inspiretoact.com.

Inspire To Act

With Our Thanks and Gratitude

*"As we express our gratitude, we must never forget
that the highest appreciation is not to utter words,
but to live by them."
- John F. Kennedy*

We are incredibly blessed with healthy families,
wonderful friends and a dedicated team of
professionals to work with every day. **Inspire to Act**
was a labor of love to write and a passion we couldn't
wait to share. Living an attitude of gratitude changes
the lives of those you touch and creates a ripple effect
that extends farther than the eye can see.

Thank you to our families, friends, employees, clients
and strategic partners. We are grateful for the
opportunity to share our passion for making a
difference.

Inspire To Act